Web Design Simplified: A Guide to HTML, CSS, Website Design & Development, Software and Programming

Bill Richards

I0470924

Legal Stuff

COPYRIGHT

Copyright © 2013 Checkmate Marketing Group LLC. All rights reserved worldwide.

No part of this publication may be replicated, redistributed, or given away in any form without the prior written consent of the author and publisher.

Checkmate Marketing Group LLC

LIMITATION OF LIABILITY

Table of Contents

Dear Readers

This book endeavors to throw light on the basics of web development and provide a thorough overview of the markup language HTML. In it you will find all you need to know about HTML, from its history to its syntax and working. If you are new to web development this book will help you hone your skills and master HTML usage and structure. Even if you have some familiarity with the HTML language you will still will find the book a helpful reference while writing HTML code.

The book is divided into five main sections. The first introduces you to HTML, its history and it use. The second gives an introduction to the working of the internet and where HTML fits into the context. There is a detailed description of HTML tags, attributes and elements. The third section deals with the concept of CSS: what it is, why we should use it and more importantly, when.. Then there is a section where different IDEs are discussed where you can develop HTML code and see how it will appear on the web. We have chosen MS FrontPage and Adobe Dream Weaver for their popularity, simplicity and availability. Then a brief introduction to web hosting and CMS will familiarize you with Joomla, Wordpress. etc.

The book is full of examples and screenshots that will help the reader understand the code better and try working on code on their own. It is written in a very simple and comprehensive way and does not require any advance knowledge of software and programming. If you have used internet only for e-mailing or social networking, you can still understand this book and start working on developing your own webpages before uploading them on the worldwide web.

HTML is the simplest web designing tool and it is prudent to start with it as your first step in the long journey to understanding programming languages, especially the ones used to design web-based applications.

We hope you enjoy reading the book and that it proves helpful and useful for you.

History and Introduction

The World Wide Web has spread its roots throughout the globe and has become a quintessential part of modern man's life. The history of HTML can be traced back through the history of the internet as it has developed alongside and is used in developing the webpages throughout the World Wide Web and giving them uniformity, readability, proper formatting and an aesthetically pleasing appearance. In fact the very first step towards web development is to acquire some familiarity with HTML.

1.1 What is HTML

HTML stands for Hypertext Markup Language. As the name indicates it is a markup language comprised of mark up tags that are always enclosed in angle brackets <> and are almost always used in pairs having a starting and ending tag. Here the question arises: what is a markup language? A markup language is one that determines different aspects of how a document will look like irrespective of what text is in it.

HTML markup tags annotate the webpages so that they are syntactically distinguished from the textual content. It is a very simple and easy language and is used to develop simple and static WebPages. To build the pages, dynamic scripts are embedded inside the HTML code.

—

1.2 History of HTML

Like the internet, HTML is not an ancient phenomenon. When the internet was expanding during the early nineties, there was a need to define a standard for webpages that the browsers could understand. Like the internet, the birth of HTML also took place at CERN. Tim Berners-Lee, the creator of the internet, a contractor at CERN, produced the first form of HTML and wrote server and browser side codes. In 1991, his HTML (called HTML tags) became publically available and at that time it had only eighteen elements. HTML has gone through a number of upgrades and changes since then, keeping in view the expanding and evolving nature of the internet and websites. A number of newer versions of HTMLHTML were developed. In 1997 a milestone was achieved when the w3 consortium recognized HTML 3.2 as an HTML cross industry standard so that all browsers and web page reader applications could follow one main prototype. These days HTML 5 has also made it into the mainstream and is quite popular. With each new version the developers try to separate the text from the syntax of the page appearance.

Let's begin our learning process and plunge into the world of web design and HTML programming.

The Internet and Web Design

Let us start by providing a brief overview of how the internet works so that you can better understand the subtleties behind web design. The internet is a gigantic repository of information on every topic and aspect imaginable. It comprises a number of networks of computers joined together by various communication modes. Where is this large amount of data stored? How does it get on our computer screens within seconds of sending a request? Where do our requests go? These and a lot of other questions naturally pop into the mind of internet users.

Here we will present to you the work of this complicated network in a simple and easy-to-understand manner.

2.1 Internet

The data on the internet is stored in the form of millions and millions of web pages. These pages are stored on machines all around the globe. The machines that store the pages are called servers. Each machine is identified by a unique name called an IP address that is a series of digits.

Domain names took over for IP addresses in the 1990s since they were much easier to use. Domain names come in a format of numbers and letters separated by dots, like www.example.com. This was a much better format to use.

The next big breakthrough came in the form of DNS or the Distributed Name Service. This is how domain names were mapped to IP addresses. This made e-mail, website domain names and the internet in general much more accessible and easier to use.

The following figure explains how it works in a simple way

The working of the internet

The client requests a page through a unique address called URL (Universal Resource Locator) through a web browser. This request goes through different routers to the web server that retrieves the page from the database server and sends it back to the requesting client's computer.

2.2 Web design

The internet is the largest repository of information in the world. To make the information readable and organized, web pages have to follow certain norms and rules so that they are uniform to an extent and conform to the requirements of the servers. Every web page has certain more or less common elements. Two very important features on a web page are its navigational feasibility and visual appeal. The webpage must have working links to other pages of the website and to its homepage. These links must be prominently placed so that they are easily accessible to the client. The page must be designed in a way that is appealing to the eyes and does not pose a problem when reading the content. Also, the page must not be cluttered with too much information and the content must be properly organized. The color scheme is also a very important aspect of the page. Choose the color scheme based on the target audience (bright for children, normal for adults, etc) and the subject matter that is covered on the pages.

A webpage has two types of elements: perceived elements and internal elements.

Perceived elements

These are the elements that the client can see on screen when he is viewing the page. It consists of the material that provides information regarding a topic. It has texts, images, charts and graphs included in it. It can also have interactive information like feedback forms and buttons. Another important part of the perceived elements are the hyperlinks and links to other websites.

Internal elements

These are elements present on the original page but which will not be shown by the browser to the end user. This includes metadata. The metadata is the header of the webpage. The header also includes the page name and title. Then it includes comments – the remarks from the programmer of the page. The scripts and HTML tags are also internal to the webpage.

 Let us take the example of a very well-known and commonly used web page and study its different parts and structure.

A web page (www.google.com)

The web page above is one of the most commonly used search engine. It is an interactive page since it has text field and buttons. The top shows the menu which provides navigational options.

Introduction to HTML

Now that we have a basic understanding of the working of the internet and knowledge about what websites and web pages are, let's move forward to the development phase. Creating a web page is a very interesting and creative thing and there are a myriad of varied options available. You can experiment with colors, styles, fonts, images, etc. and create something that is esthetically balanced and easy to use. The first step of this interesting and innovative journey is to learn HTML.

3.1 How HTML works

HTML is processed on the client's end. The browser that the end user is using has the ability to read HTML and display pages according to it. Hence when a browser receives a page in response to its request, it processes its HTML and then displays the contents according to the specifications. HTML is not displayed in the browser, but the text that is displayed is according to the instructions embedded in the HTML tags on the page. (To view the HTML of a webpage go to the "Tools" option in the browser menu and select "view source",) It is part of the hidden elements of the webpage.

You can edit HTML pages by using professional HTML editors like CoffeeCup HTML Editor, Adobe Dreamweaver or Microsoft Expression Web. But for beginners we recommend a simpler text editor like WordPad or Notepad++ (Windows) or TextEdit (Mac). These are readily available and are a good way to learn HTML because in professional editors the number of options, suggestions and auto-fill options will result in the user not completely knowing certain things. HTML pages have the extension '.HTML'. Create a Notepad file. Save it with .HTML extension and voila! You are ready to begin coding.

3.2 Basics about HTML

HTML is written in the form of tags. The tags are enclosed in angle brackets like <body></body>. The first one is known as the starting tag and the second is the ending tag. The ending tag has a forward slash that distinguishes it from the starting tag. The tag names are representative of their purpose and functionality. For example, a body tag's name indicates that inside it the main content of the page is displayed. Mostly the tags come in pairs but there are a few exceptions that we will see later in the book where a single tag is sufficient.

The tag names are not case sensitive but there is a naming convention – it is supposed to be written in lower case. We also will adapt this practice in all the examples given in this book.

HTML elements

HTML elements are a very important part of the language. Some people confuse them with HTML tags or use them interchangeably, but they are different. An HTML element is everything from the beginning of a tag to its end tag. It includes the tag, its attributes and the text between the starting and ending tags. For example, it can be written like this:

<tag>   **Element content</tag>**

This whole line of code is called an HTML element. Thus the tags are a part of the HTML element. If there is no content in an element, it is called an empty element. The most commonly used empty element is <br>. It gives a line break wherever you put it.

HTML attributes

 Attributes are another important part of an HTML element. The attribute defines the characteristics of an element. For example:

<p id="para1">this is a paragraph </p>

Here id is the attribute and para1 is its value. Attributes are always written as

Attribute name = "attribute value"

Writing the value in quotes is not necessary but considered a good programming practice. o it is better to adopt it.

Different HTML elements can have different attributes but following are some attributes that can be applied to any element:

Attribute Explanation

class	Denotes an element's class name which refers to the CSS.
id	Denotes an element's unique id.
style	Denotes an element's inline CSS styling.
title	Denotes an explanation of the element it is attached to as a tool tip.

3.3 HTML document structure

Now that we have learnt about tags, attributes and elements it is the right time to know about what a basic HTML page looks like. In the following example we take a basic HTML page and then discuss its various components.

<head>

<title> page name</title>

</head>

<body>

<p>This is my first HTML page.</p>

</body>

</HTML>

Every HTML page begins with <!DOCTYPE HTML>. This specifies that it is an HTML document and the browser must process it accordingly. Then comes the HTML starting tag. All the components on the page lie between the HTML elements. It begins at the top of the page and ends at the bottom.

Then comes the header element. The header can contain the name of the page, title, etc. Sometimes the head also has metadata information. The body is another very important tag as it contains the content to be displayed to the end user in the browser window. <p> is the paragraph element and when the <p> ends the browser automatically opens a new paragraph. At the end is the end tag of the body and after that the HTML tag is finally closed. Always close the tag when you open it.

When an element contains another element inside it, this is called element nesting. HTML pages are usually heavily nested in one main tag like HTML or body tags. You can write this code in a notepad file, save the file with an HTML extension and then open it in a browser. You will see your very first web page on the screen.

HTML Tags and Their Attributes

Now let us look at different HTML tags, their attributes and functionality. To start with, we will mention the ones easiest to use and most frequently required.

4.1 HTML Headings tags

HTML has six headings tags: <h1>, <h2> to <h6>. The <h1> tag is the one which has the largest font; the font size decreases from <h1> to <h6> in that order. You must use headings tags on your webpage for important sections because search engines and web crawlers index your pages by headings. Also, users skim through headings to know whether a page has information they need or not, so headings are very important.

Example:

<h1> Here is how to format a heading for H1 tags </h1>

<h2> Here is how to format a heading for H2 tags </h2>

<h3> Here is how to format a heading for H3 tags </h3>

<h4> Here is how to format a heading for H4 tags </h4>

<h5> Here is how to format a heading for H5 tags </h5>

<h6> Here is how to format a heading for H6 tags </h6>

Try out this example to see the difference between different headings and their formats in your browser. Browsers automatically add some empty space (a margin) before and after each heading.

4.2 HTML comments tag

Comments are very important in the code to increase its readability for future changes and updates. However, the browser ignores them and they are not displayed to the user. They are written mainly for the developer's benefit. The syntax of comments is as follows:

<!— Here's a comment -->

It is a single tag with no forward slash in it.

4.3 HTML Line and paragraph tags

Both these tags are used to increase the readability of text and make it more organized. The line tag <hr> creates a line on a web page. It can be used to separate different contents. It is used as a single tag.

<hr>

Paragraph tags <p></p> show what makes up a paragraph from a piece of text.

<p>This is a paragraph.</p>

`<p>This is another paragraph</p>`

It is also possible to give a line break with using the paragraph tag. `<br>` is the tag for it and there is no end tag for `<br>`. It is single tag element or empty element. Using the paragraph and br tags together we get

`<p>This is<br>a para<br>graph with line breaks</p>`

4.4 HTML formatting tags

A lot of formatting options are available in HTML to make your text look and appear as you want. `<b>` is to make text bold and `<i>` makes it italic, and `<sub>` and `<sup>` tags make it superscript and subscript.

For example:

`<!DOCTYPE HTML>`

`<HTML>`

```
<body>

<b>This will appear bold</b>

This appears as a <sub>subscript</sub> and this will appear
as a <sup>superscript</sup>

<strong>This will appear strong</strong>

<i>This will appear in italics</i>

<em>This will appear emphasized</em>

<code>This will appear as computer output</code>

</body>

</HTML>
```

The <em> and <strong> tags are used to lay an emphasis on
text. <strong> usually makes the text bold and <em> makes it
italic.

4.5 HTML hyperlinks

Links or hyperlinks are most important on a web page to make it connect to the rest of the website. The anchor tag, written as <a>, is used to define a link. It can be text, image, etc. When a cursor moves over it by default it is turned into a hand and in some cases the link gets highlighted or the color changes.

Most browsers have the following characteristics for links that can be overridden through attributes:

Links that appear in blue and are underlined are unvisited;

Links that are underlined and appear purple have been visited;

Active links appear underlined and in red.

Example:

<ahref="http://www.google.com/">Visit google</a>

This piece of code will appear in the browser as a link Visit google. It will take you to the google homepage.

The anchor tag cannot work without the href attribute. The href attribute describes where the link will be directed to once it is clicked.

Another useful attribute of anchor tags is the target attribute. The target attribute lets you open the document in a new window or new tab. You have to set a target ="_blank" to make it open in a new window or tab depending on which browser you are using.

The id attribute is also very useful as it helps in creating bookmarks in the same document. So if you have a very long document and you want to go to a specific section in it, you can give the id of the section in the href attribute and the link will take you to that specific section.

For example:

<a id="tips"> This is an important tips part </a>

This will create a link to the important tips part:

<ahref="#tips">Click Here to visit the important tips part</a>

This will link to the important tips part from another webpage:

<ahref="http://www.urlexample.com/page.htm#tips">

Click here for important tips</a>

4.6 HTML head tags

One of the most important elements is the head element. It is where you add elements such as: the page title, scripts, css styling, metadata, and more. This is how each one works:

Tag	Explanation
<head>	Specifies document information.
<title>	Specifies the page title to appear.
<base>	Specifies the link target that is the default for links on the

page.

<link>   Specifies how the external target relates to the current page.

<meta>   Specifies the page's metadata.

<script>   Specifies the scripts that run client-side.

<style>   Specifies the page styling to appear.

4.7 HTML div tags

The div is an abbreviation of division and as the name indicates, the div tag is used to divide the HTML page into groups and parts to increase its readability and organize the page. The different divisions are given different background colors or different font styles to make them unique.

For example:

```
<div style="color:#0000FF">
  <h3>This is a heading</h3>
  <p>This is a paragraph.</p>
</div>
<div style="color:#0000EE">
  <h3>This is a heading</h3>
  <p>This is a paragraph.</p>
</div>
```

The above example creates two divisions on the page with different colors.

There are also other elements in HTML. The complete list can be found on the internet. They are simple to use and embed in your code. The browser adds a break before and after the div element.

Cascading Style Sheets

Cascading Style Sheets is shortened to CSS. The programming language is used to define the format and visual elements on a webpage. CSS adds styling to the markup language. The most popular use is in HTML pages, but it can also be used in other markup languages.

CSS is used to simplify the programming it takes to create a webpage. Instead of including presentation elements in every page, one main CSS document can be used. The elements that CSS affects include elements like fonts, spacing, layouts, text elements, background colors, etc. CSS is also used to dynamically adjust webpages to the screen size of the device it is being displayed on.

Why is it called the cascading style sheets? The answer is simple and tells something very important about the nature of CSS. The style which is applied to an element is through a priority scheme. If more than one rule matches against an element priorities and weights are calculated and assigned to different rules and the result is according to that priorities.

Many versions of CSS are available ranging from CSS 1 to CSS 4 and some others too. Different browsers parse the CSS differently so the output of same code maybe different in different browsers but the differences will not be that significant.

There are three main styles in which we can use CSS 1) Inline styling 2) Internal styling and 3) External styling

5.1 Inline Styles

In inline style the attribute style is used in HTML elements. This attribute can set a number of styling and formatting attributes of the element.

For example if we want to apply a specific formatting to a paragraph we set its attributes as follows:

This is a paragraph with formatting.

This formatting will be applied to this paragraph only and its scope will finish with the ending tag </p>. this will change the color of the font of paragraph to blue and will have a margin of 20 pixels from the left.

Now let us look at the style options individually. The most commonly used is the background color. You can set the background color of the webpage through this attribute.

Example

```
<!DOCTYPE HTML>
<HTML>
<body style="background-color:yellow;">
</body>
</HTML>
```

This will set the background color of your page to blue. You can highlight different parts of the page by giving them different background colors.

For example

```
<body style="background-color:blue;">
<p style="background-color:yellow;">Here is the 1st paragraph to appear</p>
```

```
<p style="background-color:white;">Here is the 2nd
paragraph to appear</p>
</body>
```

The example above provides a page with a blue background
but the 1st and 2nd paragraphs will appear with yellow and
white background colors.

The next attribute is alignment. Alignment is used to display
the text in the center, right or left positions as is needed. Here
is an example:

```
<body>
<h2 style="text-align:left;">This text is aligned to the
left</h2>
<p>Here is a paragraph after the heading</p>
</body>
```

The heading will appear aligned to the left here.

Font family attribute

Setting up the font style is done using font color, font style
and font size wherever it is added to the page. This one font
attribute can add several styling properties. Here is an
example:

```
<body>
<p style="font-family: Times New Roman;color:blue;font-
size:12px;">This is the text for the paragraph. </p>
</body>
</HTML>
```

This will apply the font style, font size and font color to the
paragraph text.

5.2 Selectors and Declaration

At this point it is essential to introduce some more important concepts regarding CSS. CSS rules consist of two main parts: the selectors and a declaration. For example, if we are to define a rule for the formatting of <p> element, it is written like this:

P {color:red;text-align:center;}

Here P is called the selector and text between the {} are two declarations of p. Each declaration has two parts: property and value of the attribute, like in our example – color and text-align are properties and the values are reed and center. A declaration must end with a ;.

It is not necessary what selectors are predefined HTML elements. CSS allows us to define our own selectors. There are two types of these selectors: first is the id and the second is class

Id selectors

The id selector is used to define an element that has an id which is the same as the name of the id selector. As ids are unique, this selector will apply to only one HTML element. The name of the id selector must start with the '#' sign.

Example:

#styledelement
{
text-align:center;
color:red;
}

Class selector

The class selector defines CSS rules for all HTML elements whose class attribute has the same value as the name of the class selector. The class selector name must start with the '.'

Example:

.center {text-align:center;}

In this example, wherever the class attribute's name will be centered, the text will be center aligned.

You can play around with selectors in a number of ways. If a number of selectors have the same declaration they can be grouped together in comma-separated lists. For example, if you want all your headings to be red-colored, you can declare the selector as follows:

H1,h2,h3,h4,h5,h6

{color:red;}

Another thing that we can do with selectors is nesting. For example, if we declare an element and then declare the same element again with a pseudo class, the browser will first check the class attributes value. If it is the same then the formatting rules in the pseudo class will be applied to it, if not the type class declaration will be used.

```
<!DOCTYPE HTML>
<HTML>
<head>
<style>
p
{
color:red;
text-align:left;
}
```

```
.marked
{
background-color:blue;
}
.marked p
{
color:black;
}
</style>
</head>
<body>
<p>This text in the paragraph is left aligned and appears
red.</p>
<div class="marked">
<p>The text in this paragraph is not red.</p>
</div>
<p>p elements appearing within a class "marked" element
retain the alignment styling but the text color is different.</p>
</body>
</HTML>
```

Attribute selectors

Another type of selectors are the attribute selectors that can be applied to a specific attribute. For example, the following rule will be applied to all the elements with the title attribute.

```
[title]
{
color:blue;
}
```

However it is more commonly used in attributes and value pairs. If an attribute has a certain value, then the rule applies. For example:

```
[title="Chapter 2"]
```

```
{
color:blue;
}
```

Here the text color will be blue only if the title of the element is Chapter 2. In some cases the names may be case sensitive, in others not.

Now that these basic rules and definitions are clear, we proceed to the internal and external styles and their benefits.

5.3 Internal Styles

In internal styles the element <style> is used. It is embedded inside the <head> element and its scope is throughout the page. Internal style is used to save the time and effort of repeatedly writing the same code. Once a style is defined in the header of the page, you can apply it to any number of elements on the page by using its name. However, the scope of internal styles is only throughout the page whose header has its declaration and not on other pages of the same site.

Example:

```
<!DOCTYPE HTML>
<HTML>
<head>
<style>
body
{
background-color:#d0eeee;
}
h1
{
color:orange;
text-align:center;
}
```

```
p
{
font-family:"Arial";
font-size:12px;
}
</style>
</head>
<body>
<h1>CSS magically applies styling</h1>
<p>The first example of internal styling.</p>
<h1>CSS magically applies styling again here</h1>
<p>The second example of internal styling.</></p>
</body>
</HTML>
```

This example though it seems confusing is pretty simple and straightforward. Here we have defined formatting for the body, h1 and paragraph elements in the head element of the page. In the body we have used these elements twice and each time they will be formatted according to the definition in the head element of the page.

5.4 External styles

In external styles the CSS is written in a separate file and to use it on a page we have to include its reference on that page. This is considered the best form of styling as it completely disassociates the styling with the content. Also it can be included in any number of files so the same formatting can be applied to various pages without the hassle of writing the code again and again increasing the efficiency of the code

It also reduces the chances of error in formatting while trying to make two pages similar. In the separate CSS file the classes are defined for each element whose formatting needs to be defined.

For example, taking the same example used previously, the code defined in the header will be written in a separate file with .css extension. Then you can include its reference on any number of pages you like.

To link the file, use the <link> tag in the head element of the page. The syntax is as follows:

```
<head>
<link type="text/css" rel="stylesheet" href="style.css">
</head>
```

Using the link tags is how one can specify the relationship of the external resource to the document page.

However, the main utility of the external style sheets is that you can define your own new pseudo classes that are not already existing tags and apply them to the HTML elements.

HTML Forms and HTML Entities

HTML has made creating and updating forms very easy and feasible. Forms come under the umbrella of interactive content as they get the user's response and process data accordingly then sends it back to the server. The server then contacts the database and performs the action as required.

To make a form, a <form> tag is used. Always use form tags to enclose input elements so that the server can know that they belong as a single entity. If a page has more than one form, make sure you enclose the input from each in its respective parent form.

The forms usually contain special types of elements called the input elements that include text fields, buttons, labels, password fields, etc. In this chapter we first determine the different kinds of input elements then make a form with them.

6.1 Input element

<input> is a single tag element and does not require an ending tag. The input elements are part of the form and can be of many different types like checkboxes, radio buttons, text boxes, text area or password fields depending on the type attribute of the input element.

Text field

For example to get a text field we will set the type attribute to "text." For example, the following code asks for the first and second name of people.

```
<form action="form_demo.asp">

Your First Name Here <input value="Enter first name here" type="text"name="first-name" >

<br/>

Your Last Name Here<input value="Enter last name here" type="text" name="last-name">

<br/>

<input value="Submit" type="submit" >

</form>
```

Password input fields are similar to the text input fields with one major difference: the letters or numbers that are inputted show as circles '*' to hide the password. Here is how it appears in HTML:

```
<form>

Your Password<input name=" password " type="password" >

</form>
```

If you need a form that provides only a few options to answer a question, such as a survey, then check boxes can be used. Here is an example:

```
<form>

<input value="Bike" name="transportation-mode" type="checkbox" >I want a car<br>

<input value="Car" name="transportation-mode" type="checkbox" >I want a motorcycle

</form>
```

If the person does not own a car or a bike then he can leave both the checkboxes empty. If you want an option to be selected by default, then you can write the word checked in it to make it a default choice. Like this:

```
<input type="checkbox" name="vehicle" value="Bike" checked>I have a bike<br>
```

Here the value bike will be checked by default when the user loads the form. The user has the option to uncheck it.

Radio buttons

Radio button input option is used when the user is supposed to choose only one option from a predetermined set of options. One option from the radio button has to always be selected and it cannot remain empty.

```
<form>

<input value="no" name="unit" type="radio" >No<br>

<input value="yes" name="unit" type="radio" >Yes<br>
```

```
<inputvalue="Prefer    Not    To    Answer"    name="unit"
type="radio" >Prefer Not To Answer<br>
```

```
</form>
```

Text area

Text area is also an input type text field which allows you to write a large number of multiline text. It has the text scrolling option also that makes it suitable in forms where descriptions are required. The text can be of unlimited size but it is usually limited by adding a maximum length attribute. Also it can be limited by specifying a columns and rows attribute that will restrict the length of the text to maximum number of rows and columns.

```
<textareacols="25" rows="5" >
```

Here is a text area. It holds lots of text. This is more text in the text area. So here is more text for the text area. And this is even more text for the text area.

```
</textarea>
```

Submit button

The next input type is the submit button. Every form must have a submit button to send the data to the server that will then consult the data base. The submit button is usually at the bottom of the page at the end of the form. The data is sent to the file in the form's action attribute.

The following example shows how to take data from two text fields and send it to the file myData when the submit button is pressed.

```
< !DOCTYPE HTML >

<HTML>

<body>

<form method="get"action="data.asp" name="input" >

First name: <input value="john" type="text"  name = "first-name" ><br>

Last name: <input value="Doe" type="text"  name = "last-name" ><br>

<inputvalue="Submit" type="submit" >

</form>
```

```html
<p>When the "Submit" button is clicked, the inputs will be
sent to "data.asp".</p>

</body>

< /HTML >
```

If you click the "Submit" button, the form data will be sent to a
page called "mydata.asp".

In this way we can use different input types to make a
complex form. Forms can also have drop-down lists and
menus that we will explain in coming chapters.

HTML entities

HTML entities are special combinations of characters that
represent reserved characters in HTML. In HTML there are
some reserved words that we cannot write in the content as
they can be confused with HTML code by the browser. For
example, we cannot use starting and ending angle brackets <
or >. The reason is that the while parsing the code the browser
might take them as tags so in order to write these special
characters we use a special sequence that is called a character
entity. The entity starts with a & sign or &# sign followed by
the entity name. So in order to display less than sign we write
< or <

A very commonly used character entity is for giving empty space on a web page and is written as . The browser ignores the spaces given in code so in order to give space this character entity is used.

Following is the list of HTML character entities available:

Character	Explanation	Character Number	Character Number
©	Copyright	&#169;	&#169;
	non-breaking space		
&	Ampersand	&#38;	&#38;
™	Trademark	&#8482;	&#8482;
®	registered trademark	&#174;	&#174;
£	Pound	&#163;	&#163;
¥	Yen	&#165;	&#165;

€	Euro	&#8364;	&#8364;
<	less than	&#60;	&#60;
¢	Cent	&#162;	&#162;
>	greater than	&#62;	&#62;
§	Section	&#167;	&#167;

Images, Tables and Lists

In this chapter we discuss some advanced HTML concepts that are commonly used in web programming and that are mainly concerned with uncluttering the look of the website and giving it an appealing feel. First we'll discuss images.

7.1 HTML images

Images have become an essential part of websites. It is said that a picture is worth a thousand words and this is especially true in the virtual world because with hundreds of pages on a single topic available, people lose interest in one page very soon and they need to know at a glance what the page has to offer. To keep people hooked and ensure their returning again to your web page it is necessary to beautify your page with relevant and aesthetically pleasing pictures. HTML manages images with the <img> tag. The img tag is single and does not need an ending tag. It only works on its attributes.

The image tag's most important attribute is imgsrc which determines the location of the image from where the image needs to be uploaded. src means source.

Syntax for defining an image:

```
<imgalt="tex here"src="imageurl" >
```

The URL points to the location where the image is stored. The image is loaded from the server every time the page request is sent so it is necessary that the image files stay on the location that is mentioned in the imgsrc value. If the image is not there, the user gets a broken link error.

The alt attribute is for situations where the image is not available. Its value contains the text that will be displayed if for some reason the image is not available for display. Always use the alt attribute because for many reasons, situations may arise where you cannot display the image.

Images can use width and height attributes. Many people consider it a best practice to include both. If they are not included then the image will appear as the actual size of the image file. This can negatively affect the page layout. Here is an example:

```
<imgsrc="url"    alt="this    is    an    image."    width="304"
height="228">
```

Use images only where they are required. No need to clutter the page with unnecessary images that are of no relevance to the page. Also, you need to remember that the more images there are the more bandwidth is required for page loading and efficiency of the loading may be decreased, which can ultimately discourage the user from visiting your page. So it is necessary to use images thoughtfully and not throw them in randomly.

Images as links

Sometimes we need to make images as links, so that when a user clicks on them he/she is directed to a new page. This is especially needed when making websites for kids or for illiterate people. To make an image a link, it is given in the content art of the anchor tag of an element.

```
<!DOCTYPE HTML>

<HTML>

<body>

<p>Image link created here:

<a href="www.facebook.com">

<img width="40" height="40" src="imageurl" alt="image alt text" ></a></p>
```

```
<p>Image with no border but with a link still:

<a href="www.facebook.com">

<img width="40" height="40" border="0" src="imageurl"
alt="image alt text" ></a></p>

</body>

</HTML>
```

Here is an example. In it you just have to give the address of the image that are making a link in of the url section. It will be an ordinary-looking image but the cursor will become a hand once it hovers over it.

Here it should be noted that image alignment was earlier a big issue but in the new HTML 5 this and its associative tags are depreciated and is done through CSS only.

Image map

It is also possible to create an image map. This is when different parts of the image are different links that will take you to different pages once clicked. The can be done by using the map tags inside the image tags. However the tricky part is that we have to give the exact co-ordinates of the image from where we want one link and from where we want another link. The co-ordinates are given in the coordinates attribute. This image map is mostly used when images of maps are uploaded and the user clicks on one area and the page with information about this area is displayed.

7.2 HTML tables

Tables are also a very important part of HTML. Usually HTML pages are all divided into tables and we work in different table cells without realizing it.

The < table > tag defines a table. Tables as you know are divided into rows and columns but in HTML there is a little difference. Inside the table tag we put a <tr> tag to represent the table rows. And within the <tr> tags are <td> tags that represent table data cells. The number of td cells in each tr tag will be equal to the number of columns that you want to add in the table. And the number of tr tags in table tags will be equal to the number of rows you want in the table. Each table data cell can contain text, images, videos and even other tables.

Here is a simple example that creates a two-by-two table with two rows and two columns.

```
<table border="1">

<tr>

<td>Here is cell 1 and row 1 of the table</td>

<td>Here is cell 2 and row 1 of the table </td>

</tr>

<tr>

<td>Here is cell 1 and row 2 of the table </td>

<td>Here is cell 2 and row 2 of the table </td>

</tr>

</table>
```

How the HTML code above looks in a browser:

Here is cell 1 and row 1 of the table	Here is cell 2 and row 1 of the table
Here is cell 1 and row 2 of the	Here is cell 2 and row 2 of the

table	table

In the above example, the table is displayed with a border of size 1. If you do not want borders to show, do not specify the border attribute; however, if you want the borders then it is necessary to specify the border attribute.

Another important aspect of tables is table headers. Table headers are the topmost data cells of each column of the table. The table header is defined by a <th> tag. The data in the th cell will be automatically bold and centered.

HTML Table Headers

It is possible to define headers in a table using the <th> tag.

Browsers will show this text as center-aligned and bold.

<table border="1">

<tr>

```html
<th>Here is table header 1</th>

<th>Here is table header 2</th>

</tr>

<tr>

<td>Here is cell 1 and row 1 of the table

</td>

<td>Here is cell 2 and row 1 of the table

</td>

</tr>

<tr>

<td>Here is cell 1 and row 2 of the table

</td>

<td>Here is cell 2 and row 2 of the table

</td>

</tr>

</table>
```

How the HTML code above looks in your browser:

Here is table header 1	Here is table header 2
Here is cell 1 and row 1 of the table	Here is cell 2 and row 1 of the table
Here is cell 1 and row 2 of the table	Here is cell 2 and row 2 of the table

7.3 Lists

Lists are used to display data that is in group form. There are two main types of lists. First is the ordered list and second is the unordered list. The ordered lists are defined by <ol> tags and unordered lists are defined by <ul> tags. Within the list the list items are defined by <li> tags.

The following example defines a very simple unordered list:

<ul>

<li>Books</li>

<li>Pencils</li>

<li>Erasers</li>

<li>Sharpeners</li>

</ul>

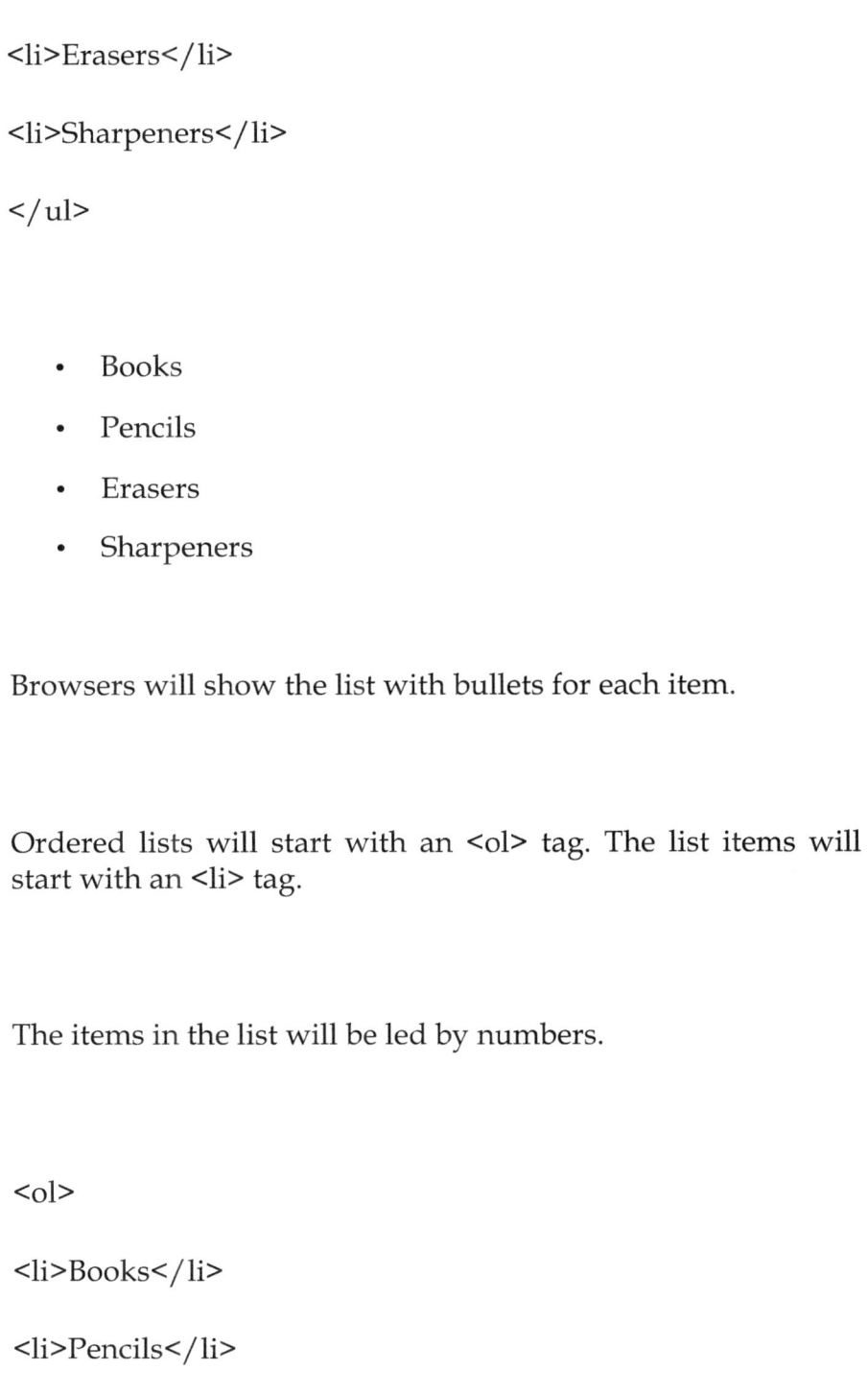

- Books
- Pencils
- Erasers
- Sharpeners

Browsers will show the list with bullets for each item.

Ordered lists will start with an <ol> tag. The list items will start with an <li> tag.

The items in the list will be led by numbers.

<ol>

<li>Books</li>

<li>Pencils</li>

```
<li>Erasers</li>

<li>Sharpeners</li>

</ol>
```

This is how the browser will display this code:

1. Books

2. Pencils

3. Erasers

4. Sharpeners

In each list item you can add another list to make it a nested list. However list nesting is a complex process and should not be done unless necessary.

Description lists

Another type of lists that are commonly used is description lists. The description lists have list items as well as a brief description of each item after it. The description list is defined by <dl> tags. The items are defined by <dt> tags and the description of each is defined in <dd> tags. This type of list is used in defining different terms or in a dictionary.

Following is an example of a simple description list:

<dl>

<dt>Tea</dt>

<dd>- A brown warm liquid to drink</dd>

<dt>Cola</dt>

<dd>- A black warm liquid to drink</dd>

</dl>

Now that we have defined complex HTML structures we can define a complete layout of an HTML page. First we make the layout of the page using the <div> and then with the <table> tags.

The following example creates a page with title pane, a content pane, a side menu pane and footer pane. We have shown each pane with a different color to differentiate between different div elements.

```
<!DOCTYPE HTML>

<HTML>

<body>

<div style="width:600px"id="container" >

<div style="background-color:#FFF000;"id="header" >

<h1>Here is the title of the webpage that appears</h1></div>

<div style="background-color:#FFF000;float:left;width:300px;height:300px;"id="menu" >

<b>Main Menu</b><br>

HTML<br>

JavaScript<br>

CSS</div>

<div id="content" style="background-color:#FFFFFF; float:left;width:200px;height:100px;">
```

Here is where the content is going</div>

```
<div        id="page       footer"       style="clear:both;text-
align:center;background-color:#FFF000;">
```

HTML Guide</div>

```
</div>
```

```
</body>
```

```
</HTML>
```

Next is the layout using the table tags. It is difficult to say which one is more difficult to use. Both require practice and understanding to master the art. However conceptually it is easier to divide the page in terms of rows and columns than considering it as separate divisions.

```
<!DOCTYPE HTML>
```

```
<HTML>
```

```
<body>
```

```
<table border="0" width="650" >
```

```
<tr>
```

```
<td colspan="2" style="background-color:#FFF000;">
```

```
<h1>Here is where you add the main webpage title</h1>

</td>

</tr>

<tr>

<td style="width:200px;background-color:# FFF000;">

<b>Main Menu</b><br>

HTML<br>

JavaScript<br>

CSS

</td>

<td          style="width:450px;height:200px;          background-color:#FFFFFF; ">

Here is where you can add content</td>

</tr>

<tr>

<td          colspan="4"          style="text-align:left;background-color:#FFF000;">

HTML Guide</td>
```

```
</tr>

</table>

</body>

</HTML>
```

Web Hosting and Content Management Systems

Now that we are able to create web pages, comes the question of how to upload them to the World Wide Web. The process of hosting web pages on the internet is very simple and all it requires is a web hosting service.

The kind of web hosting service that you require depends upon the size, type and configuration of your website. Some ISPs provide an amount of free space to store static web sites that do not require any processing done. However sites that are complex require software compatibilities of scripts and codes. Also there may be database requirements that range from little to huge.

8.1 What is web hosting?

In web hosting services the host provides server space to the client to upload their web pages onto the internet so that they can be viewed throughout the world. A lot of things come into this. Simply put, it provides a physical space to store the web pages on machines known as web servers. The computers that read the web pages are called web clients. The programs through which they are read are called web browsers – for example, Firefox, Internet Explorer, Google Chrome, Mozilla, etc. The browser sends the request through Hypertext transfer protocol (HTTP) and then displays the pages according to the display instructions on the web page.

The web hosting service providers also manage the technical aspects of maintaining a website such as keeping the database updated, keeping the information up to date, protecting from malicious attacks, etc. The space can be from one client's server or a server owned by the service provider.

8.2 Personal web hosting server

Making your own computer a server might be cheaper instead of leasing the one provided by the web hosting service provider. But then you need twenty-four hour high speed connectivity to the internet. It creates a very bad impression on the end users if they try to connect to your site and it is down, so make sure servers are always running at a good speed which means investing in high-powered hardware that can operate twenty-four hours without faltering or crashing. Such is also the case with software requirements. You will need firewalls and other protections since internet is always under the threat of being attacked by viruses, worms, Trojans, etc.

8.3 Leasing Web hosting servers

The other option is leasing a space from web hosting service providers. Here too you have to consider certain factors and requirements. Usually the ISPs provide the web hosting services and internet connection. ISP stands for internet service provider. They also provide e-mailing facility and domain name registration.

The first thing to consider in web hosting is the price package. A small personal site can be uploaded for free by an ISP however as the size and complexity of the site increases, so does its hosting costs. If it requires database support then again there will be an increase in the costs, so study the ISP's traffic volume restrictions. Make sure that you don't have to pay a fortune for unexpected high traffic if your website becomes popular. Also, if you will publish videos and large images on your site, check the ISP's bandwidth limitations. E-mail capabilities and daily backup routines are two other functionalities that must be on the checklist to determine a good ISP.

8.4 Selecting a website name

Every website must have a unique name through which the browser sends its request to the server. The name is called a URL or universal resource locator. The URL is the root address for all the web pages of the website. The main page whose exact address is the URL is called the Homepage of the website. The addresses of the other pages are appended to the URL after a forward slash.

For example if I have a website named as my website and it has three pages and the name of the website is myweb, then the homepage address will be something like this:

www.myweb.com

If the other two pages are mypictures.html and myresume.html they can be requested through the browser by writing

www.myweb.com/mypictures.html   or
www.myweb.com/myresume.html

The suffix of .com at the end of the website name stands for commercial and means that the website is for commercial use. This suffix .com is called a top-level domain as it lies at the topmost level in the domain name system of websites on the internet. The sites can have other suffixes too depending on their purpose.

.com stands for commercial but now any website can have .com as its suffix because of its wide use. Almost all websites have some sort of commercial benefit. It is one of the most popular top level domains.

,edu stands for education meaning the website is dedicated to educational purposes.

.info stands for information and means that the website is related to supplying information.

,net means network and can be used for any website connected on the net.

.org stands for organization and formerly it was made for nonprofit organizations but now it is available like .net for any website. It is again a very popular and widely used top-level domain.

Different countries also have their suffixes to denote that the site is based in a certain country like .uk for United Kingdom, .jp for Japan, .pk for Pakistan, .us for the United States of America, etc.

Choosing the proper website address is essential. The name should be concise yet descriptive of the subject matter of the site. Today with thousands and thousands of webpages strewn across the World Wide Web there is a race to reach the topmost results in all the search engines. That is why SEO has come into being and one of the foremost rules of SEO is to have a proper website name that caters to the search engine optimization. Because when the end user writes some words in the search engine the web crawler (the programs running behind search engines) looks into the site name first along with the other filtering criteria. If you choose meaningless names you will lose an important SEO option.

Also, check for the name's availability. As mentioned earlier, due to thousands of sites having the same subject matter, many good names are taken and you might be frustrated at first to see that all the names you need for your site are taken. You can have a different top-level domain to differentiate your site from others. For example, if you want to name your site myweb and www.myweb.com is already taken, try using www.myweb.org or www.myweb.net. Also, if your site is specific to your country use your country name abbreviation for that. There are websites on the internet that check for site name's availability and also give useful suggestions from available names if you specify the main theme of your website. If you want a lot of traffic to come onto your page it is better to seek the advice of a professional regarding the website name and an SEO expert for the website content. This does not cost much and gives you a lot of monetary benefit in the long run.

8.5 Types of web hosting

Here are some basic types of webhosting services. Which service to consider for your website mainly depends upon what link your website is.

Free web hosting

Many companies provide this service for small scale websites that require minimum space and maintenance capabilities. They generate the revenue through advertisement and this makes up for the free services.

Shared web hosting

Shared web hosting means sharing a single server for more than one site. This might range from a single site to a few hundred sites. All the sites share the same amount of resources like RAM from the same server. However the services that this service provides are limited. If a site becomes popular and has a large amount of traffic directed its way, then it is better to move it to a separate server.

Cloud hosting

This new type of hosting, known as cloud hosting, offers many benefits over traditional hosting. It allows customers to access resources on demand. Customers are typically only billed for the resources used, so it is a good option for sites that need access to computing resources but do not need them all the time.

8.6 Content management systems

The content management systems commonly known as CMS are hugely popular these days. These systems have made website authoring and maintaining very easy and popular even for a layman. The CMS provides an interface that is easy to use and understand. Through this interface the user can create and modify webpages. Even complex pages with images and links can be made through CMS. The CMS have the ability to design an appealing web interface. A number of content managements are available. Some popular ones are Joomla, Wordpress, Drupal, etc.

Summary

We hope that this book has helped you learn about HTML, internet and web design. This book is not aimed at making you an expert in the subject matter, which is a matter of practice and hands-on experience; however it will prove to be a guiding resource on your journey to proficiency in HTML and web design. In this book we have tried to cover topics ranging from what is the internet, what are web pages, web hosting and web servers. Then we provide knowledge in detail about the intricacies of HTML language. There are a lot of working examples in this book that will help you in writing your own code. You can change the code and play with it and manipulate it to learn more about the language. Remember, web designing is an art that should be learned with practice and hands-on experience, not just by reading a book.

We Want Your Feedback on This Book!

Our main purpose is to make sure that our readers get value from the books we publish and that they have a good experience with all of our products. We are always working to improve our books and other products with every revision and update.

Every piece of feedback makes a difference in this process. And we would appreciate yours as well - whether it is good or bad.

Please take one minute to let us know what you thought by following this link:
http://checkmatemg.com/feedbackwebdesign/

www.ingramcontent.com/pod-product-compliance
Lightning Source LLC
Chambersburg PA
CBHW071625170526
45166CB00003B/1194